GETTING TO KNOW THE WORLD'S GREATEST ARTISTS

MONET

WRITTEN AND ILLUSTRATED BY MIKE VENEZIA

CONSULTANT SARA MOLLMAN UNDERHILL

CP CHILDRENS PRESS ®

CHICAGO

For Sam Freifeld
Thanks for your ideas and encouragement

Cover: *The Houses of Parliament, Sunset.* 1903.
　　　The National Gallery of Art, Washington, D.C.

Library of Congress Cataloging-in-Publication Data

Venezia, Mike.
　　Monet / written & illustrated by Mike Venezia.
　　　　　p.　　　cm. — (Getting to know the world's greatest
artists)
　　Summary: Traces the life of the Impressionist painter
and analyzes some of his paintings.
　　ISBN 0-516-02276-8
　　1.　Monet, Claude, 1840-1926—Juvenile literature.
2.　Artists—France—Biography—Juvenile literature.
[1.　Monet, Claude, 1840-1926.　2.　Artists.
3.　Painting, French.　4.　Painting, Modern—France.
5.　Art appreciation.]　I.　Monet, Claude, 1840-1926.
II.　Title.　III.　Series.
N6847.M58V4　1989
759.4—dc20　　　　　　　　　　　　　89-25452
[B]　　　　　　　　　　　　　　　　　　　　　CIP
[92]　　　　　　　　　　　　　　　　　　　　AC

Monet Painting in his Garden at Argenteuil, 1873.
By Pierre-Auguste Renoir, Wadsworth Atheneum, Hartford, Connecticut.

Claude Monet was born in Paris,
France, in 1840. He was a great artist
and helped invent an important style
of painting called impressionism.

Many of Monet's paintings are pictures of water. Boats, oceans, ponds, and lakes were some of his favorite subjects.

Terrace at Sainte-Adresse.
The Metropolitan Museum of Art, New York

The Houses of Parliament, Sunset. 1903.
The National Gallery of Art, Washington, D.C.

Claude Monet loved the way colors
reflect in water, and the special
way that water makes the clouds and
sky look.

Monet Working in His Floating Studio Argenteuil by *Manet*
Neue Pinakothek, Munich. Scala/Art Resource

Monet even fixed up a boat as a floating studio. He kept paints, brushes, canvas, and drawing supplies on it. Monet sailed up and down rivers and streams, stopping to paint wherever he liked. It must have been fun.

When Claude Monet was little, his family moved from Paris to the town of Le Havre, which was right on the sea. At Le Havre, ships from all over the world stopped to pick up supplies

for their long journeys. Monet's father owned a grocery store that sold supplies to the sailors and shipping companies. Claude must have seen a lot of very interesting people while he was growing up.

Claude Monet had a good sense of humor, but he didn't do very well in school. He never listened to anybody, and spent most of his time drawing funny pictures. He even drew funny pictures of his teachers!

(above) *Mario Orchard*, The Art Institute of Chicago.

(top right) *Léon Marchon, Lawyer*, 1855. The Art Institute of Chicago.

(bottom right) *Caricature of a Man with a Large Nose*. 1855.
The Art Institute of Chicago.

Claude became very good at
drawing these pictures. When he
was a teenager, some people (who also
had a good sense of humor) paid him
to draw pictures of them.

Claude liked making money by selling his drawings. He kept on drawing until a well-known local artist convinced Claude he should try painting.

Eugène Boudin had some new and interesting ideas about painting that Monet liked.

Boudin thought artists should paint
outside, not in stuffy studios like
most artists did during Monet's time.

La Grenouillère, 1869. The Metropolitan Museum of Art, New York

Monet loved the idea of painting outdoors. In 1862, he left Le Havre to study art in Paris. There he met other artists. Monet made friends with Pierre-Auguste Renoir, Alfred Sisely, and Frédéric Bazille. He showed them how much fun it was to paint outdoors. Monet and his friends often painted together in the countryside.

After the invention of oil paint in
tubes, it was easier for artists to carry
their supplies around and paint outside.
Before that, artists had to mix their
own paint in jars with colored powder
and oil. It was a messy job. There
were some problems with painting
outside, though. Sometimes sand and
other things stuck to the wet paint.

Monet wanted his paintings to become well known so that people would buy them. Almost the only way he could do this was by having his paintings shown at the great Salon in Paris. The Salon was a place where people came from all over the world to see what the best artists were doing.

It wasn't easy to get a painting into the Salon. The few judges picked only the paintings they liked. Monet entered his paintings often. Sometimes they were accepted and sometimes they weren't.

Women in the Garden was one of Monet's paintings that didn't make it.

Women in the Garden, 1867.
Louvre, Paris.
Art Resource/Giraudon

Monet used his favorite model for all four women in this painting. Her name was Camille. Claude Monet and Camille fell in love and got married a few years after this painting was finished.

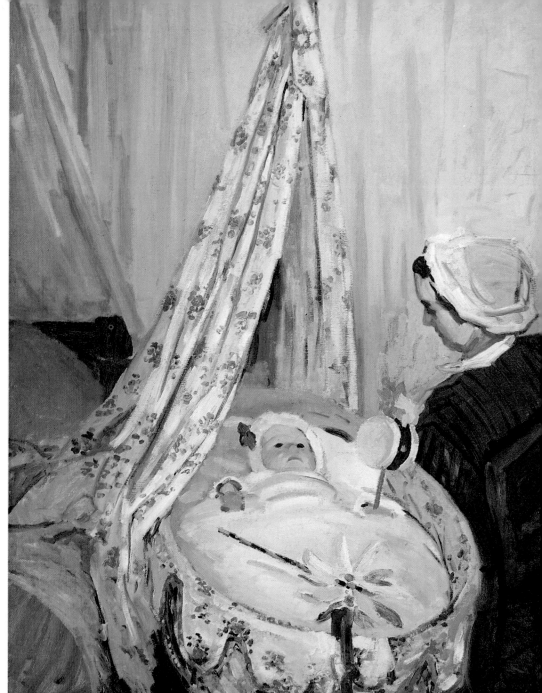

The Cradle. Camille with Jean, 1867. National Gallery of Art, Washington, D.C.

Monet often used Camille and their children as models. This is a painting of Camille and their first son, Jean.

The great Salon wasn't paying much attention to Monet and his friends, so they decided to have their own show. They wanted people to see how exciting their colorful outdoor paintings were. But the show didn't work out very well.

The Lion Hunt, by Delacroix, 1861. The Art Institute of Chicago

People in Paris in those days wanted to see paintings that told a story about some important battle or historical event. They were used to paintings where everything looked clear and sharp, and they liked dark, moody colors, like the colors in the painting above.

Impression: Sunrise, 1872. Musée Marmottan, Paris. Art Resource

Monet and his friends were more interested in how pretty something looked when the sunlight was on it. They liked to paint ordinary things, like a boat on a lake, or rocks by the ocean, or even haystacks in a field.

A newspaperman called these artists "impressionists." He got the name from Monet's painting *Impression: Sunrise.*

Even though people were not crazy about Monet's impressionist pictures, he kept on painting them. He thought it was important to show scenes of everyday life, and he tried to make the colors, shadows, and light in his paintings as real as possible. Monet was even able to show steam and dampness coming from a train engine.

Gare Saint-Lazare, 1877.
The Art Institute of Chicago

Detail of painting on Page 25

If you take a very close look at some of Monet's paintings, you can hardly tell what he painted. It just looks like a bunch of colorful brush strokes.

The Cliff Walk Pourville, 1882. The Art Institute of Chicago

But when you step back a little, it all starts to make sense. It's easy to see that the colorful brush strokes on page 24 are really the two ladies walking along a cliff in the painting above.

The Manneporte, Etretat, 1883,
The Metropolitan Museum of Art, New York

The exciting brush strokes and colors in Monet's paintings give you the feeling of being right there at the moment he made the painting.

Monet wanted to get as close as he could to the things he was painting, no matter what the conditions were. Sometimes he had to tie his easel down so that the waves wouldn't wash his painting away!

Haystacks
End of Day, Autumn
1890-91
The Art Institute
of Chicago

Monet often painted many pictures of the same thing. He wanted to see how sunlight changed the look of something at different times of the day, or at different seasons of the year.

Haystacks
End of Summer, Evening
1890-91
The Art Institute
of Chicago

The Japanese Footbridge, 1899. The Philadelphia Museum of Art

When Monet was older, people finally started to appreciate his paintings. He settled down in the French town of Giverny, and built a wonderful water garden there.

Water Lilies, 1919-1926. Cleveland Museum of Art

Claude Monet lived to be 86 years old. He spent the last ten years of his life painting scenes of his water garden. These paintings are among the most beautiful and famous paintings he did. Some of them are over forty feet wide!

Panel of Water Lily Decorations, Musée d l'Orangerie, Paris Giraudon/Art Resource

Snow at Argenteuil, Museum of Fine Arts, Boston

Monet was able to show how things looked at the moment he saw them, almost like a camera does.

He loved nature and he painted with colors so that a scene would look as much like nature as possible. He was even able to paint mist and fog and make it look real.

Venice the Grand Canal, 1908. Museum of Fine Arts, Boston

It's a lot of fun to see a real Monet painting, especially up close. You'll be surprised by how many different colors you can see and how simple Monet's brush strokes are.

The paintings in this book came from the museums listed below. If none of these museums is close to your home, maybe you can visit one when you are on vacation.

The Art Institute of Chicago, Chicago, Illinois
Cleveland Museum of Art, Cleveland, Ohio
Louvre, Paris, France
The Metropolitan Museum of Art, New York, New York
Musée Marmottan, Paris, France
Musée d'l'Orangerie, Paris, France
Museum of Fine Arts, Boston, Massachusetts
The National Gallery of Art, Washington, D.C.
Neue Pinakothek, Munich, Germany
The Philadelphia Museum of Art, Philadelphia, Pennsylvania
Wadsworth Atheneum, Hartford, Connecticut